This book belongs to

A WORLD OF NUMBERS

Written by Frances Gilbert
Illustrated by Sharon Rentz

Greene Bark Press, Inc.

Publisher's Cataloging-In-Publication Data
(Prepared by The Donohue Group, Inc.)

Gilbert, Frances.
   A world of numbers / written by Frances Gilbert ; illustrated by Sharon Rentz.

      p. : ill. ; cm.

   ISBN: 1-880851-76-8

1. Number concept--Juvenile poetry. 2. Children's poetry, American. 3. Number concept. I.
Rentz, Sharon. II. Title.

QA141.3 .G55 2005
513/.2

For Harriet

Counting
is what comes after

Daddy's thumb is one
and what come after
are Daddy's fingers
two, three, four

then what comes after
on that hand
is five

you can't say ten
until six, seven,
eight and nine
fingers are done

then ten
is what comes after

F.G.

For Travis
and Andrew
2 boys, pure joy

S.R.

zero
nothing
none
not one

some people say
'0' for zero
like in 3, 6, 0, 1
but Granny says
nought

which means
zero
nothing
none
not one

0   zero

one is one
just one
on its own
by itself
one is not
some or many
or few

one is
just one
just me
or just you

1 one

Granny says two
is a collection
you can start a collection
with two
more than one
but not quite many

two can be a collection

2 two

three
three is three rejoicing
Sandy, Jessica and me
three rejoicing

three
like a piece of an eight
that got away
three is a joyful number

3 three

four is what we are
Mama, Daddy,
brother and me
four can be
two grown ups and two children
or
three dark and one fair
or
one blue eyes and three brown

any way you count us
we are four

4 four

for a group you need five
five together make a group
five can work together
four is too tight
six is too many
five is what you need
for a group

5 five

six
so easy to say
so easy to make
curl around and tuck in tight
six is a just right number
six puppies
six apples
six ducks
six cookies
six is a just right number

6 six

seven is an awkward number

too many for round the table
unless someone gets a corner
five short of a dozen,
one more than half a dozen
so not a good number for
eggs or bagels

more than a few but not quite many
seven is an awkward number

7 seven

8 eight

you need eight
spoons & forks
for supper
four sets of two
two each for four

even when baby
drops his on the floor
it's still eight

nine

nine is a waiting number
nine
waiting to
be ten
forgets
eight, seven,
six, five, four,
three, two, one
nine is nine

almost ten

9 nine

ten is a tidy number
ten arranges itself neatly
five and five
two, two, two, two, two
six and four, eight and two
but sometimes ten gets all lopsided
seven and three, nine and one
and you have to make it neat again

10 ten

eleven

sits between ten and twelve
eleven
pairs up unevenly
is never enough
for a dozen
has no shape

eleven is a
shapeless number

11 eleven

today we made a batch of
gingerbread men
we made twelve
and laid them in
two straight rows of six
on the baking sheet
one batch of gingerbread men

batch is a good word,
round and fat
like the gingerbread men

12 twelve